Living or Not

Written by Sandra Iversen

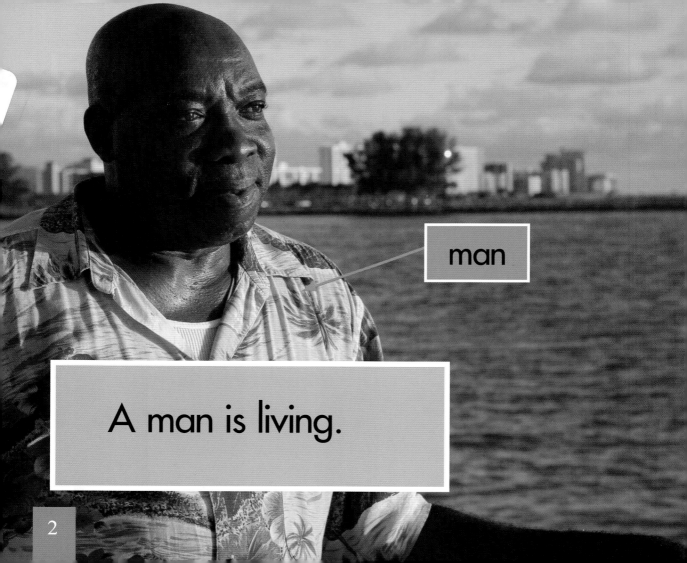

man

A man is living.

hat

A hat is not.

3

cat

A cat is living.

4

bag

A bag is not.

ram

A ram is living.

van

A van is not.

rat

A rat is living.

fan

A fan is not.

dad

A dad is living.

ham

A ham is not.

Living or Not

	Living	Not Living
cat	√	
dad	√	
fan		√
hat		√